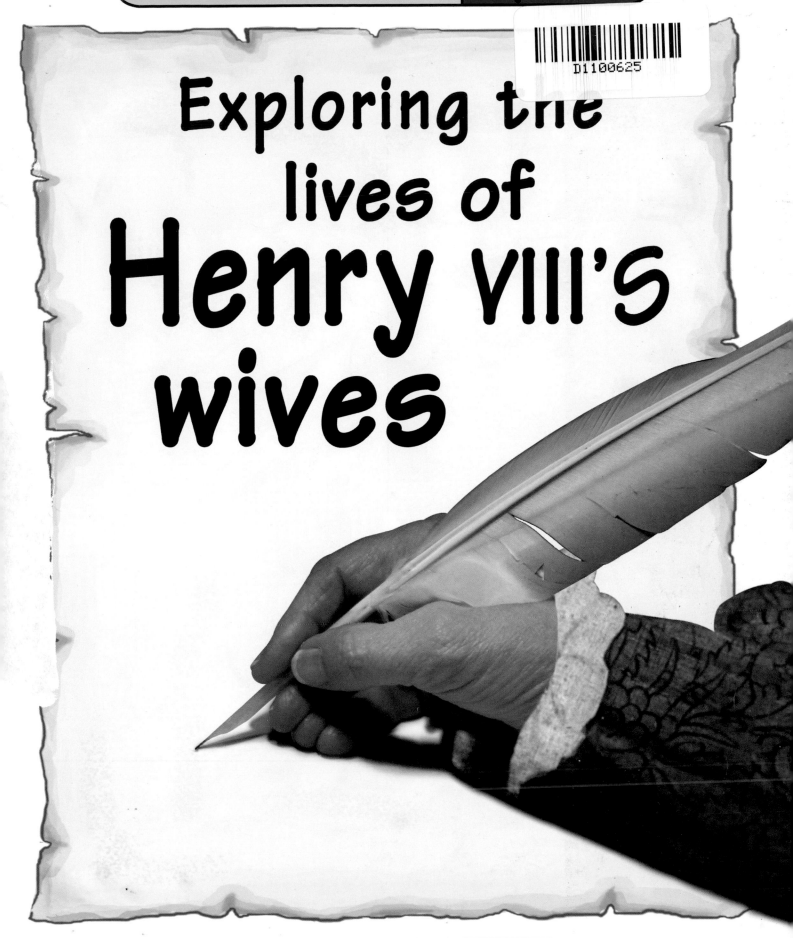

Exploring the lives of Henry VIII's wives

Dr Brian Knapp and Lisa Magloff

You can easily remember what happened to each of Henry's wives by learning this rhyme: Divorced, Beheaded, Died, Divorced, Beheaded, Survived.

Divorced

Beheaded

Died

Divorced

Beheaded

Survived

Henry VIII's wives' timeline

1509	1529	1530	1531	1532	1533	1534	1535	1536	1537	1538

Henry VIII becomes king.

Henry begins to cut ties with Rome.

Henry divorces Catherine of Aragon.

Henry becomes Head of the Church of England.

Henry VIII marries Catherine of Aragon.

Henry VIII marries Anne Boleyn and is excommunicated by the Pope. The future Elizabeth I is born.

Anne Boleyn is beheaded. Henry marries Jane Seymour.

Jane Seymour dies afte giving birth to a son – the future Edward VI.

Tudors (1485–1603)

0   1000 AD   2000 AD

0–146 BC)

Anglo-Saxons (450–1066)

Victorians (1837–1901)

Romans (700 BC–476 AD)

Vikings (800–1066/1400)

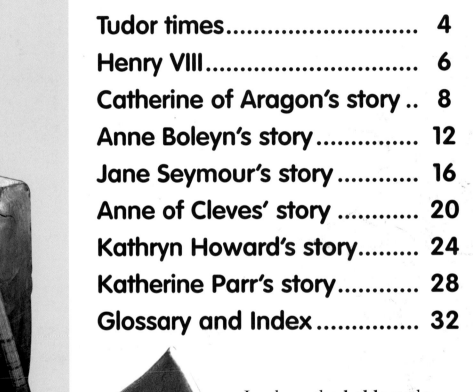

The executioner's block and axe used for beheading at the Tower of London.

Contents

Look up the **bold** words in the glossary on page 32 of this book.

Henry marries Anne of Cleves.

Kathryn Howard is beheaded.

1540   1541   1542   1543   1544   1545   1546   1547   1548   1549   1550

Henry divorces Anne of Cleves and marries Kathryn Howard.

Henry marries Katherine Parr.

Henry VIII dies. Edward VI becomes king.

Tudor times

Everyone knows that Henry VIII (Henry the eighth) had six wives. But what was it like from the wives' point of view? That is what we shall find out in this book. What you are going to read are a series of short diaries, written as though each queen is telling their life story.

Of course, they wrote about life in **Tudor** times, so to understand what they are saying, we shall start by telling you what is meant by Tudor times.

The reign of Tudor kings and queens began with Henry Tudor (1457–1509), who was Henry VII (Henry the seventh). He was the first Tudor king and Henry VIII's father.

So much power was at stake, that marriages were usually planned for the good of the country, not because people were in love. When it worked, it worked well.

The family tree on this page shows you how complicated it all was.

Henry VII (Henry Tudor).

Tudor claim to the throne

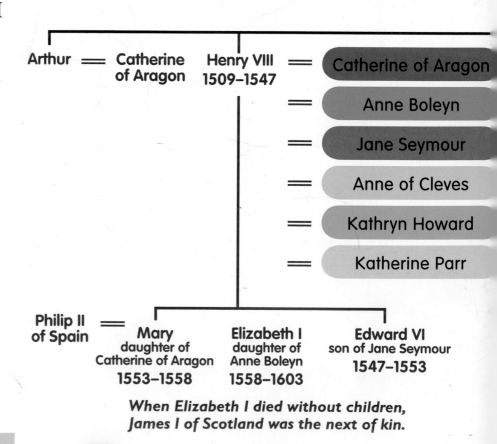

Arthur == Catherine of Aragon	Henry VIII 1509–1547 ==	Catherine of Aragon
	==	Anne Boleyn
	==	Jane Seymour
	==	Anne of Cleves
	==	Kathryn Howard
	==	Katherine Parr

Philip II of Spain ==

| Mary daughter of Catherine of Aragon 1553–1558 | Elizabeth I daughter of Anne Boleyn 1558–1603 | Edward VI son of Jane Seymour 1547–1553 |

When Elizabeth I died without children, James I of Scotland was the next of kin.

Did you know…?

- Henry VII came to power at a time when noble families of the country had been at war with each other. This is called a **civil war**. This civil war was called the Wars of the Roses.
- Henry Tudor came from the **nobles** on one side of the war – the house of Lancaster (the red rose) – and he brought peace to England by marrying Elizabeth who came from the other group of nobles in the war – the house of York (the white rose).

The Tudor Rose used the white (York) and the red (Lancaster) rose, to show that both families were now united.

 How many children did Henry VII (Henry Tudor) have?

Scotland's claim to the English throne

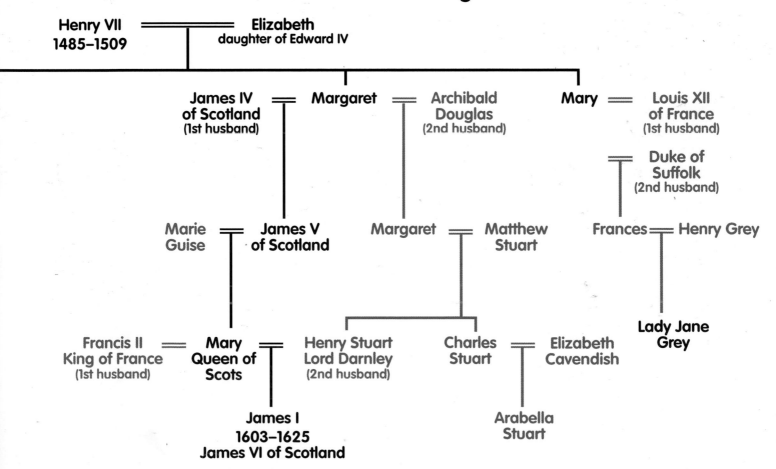

Henry VII 1485–1509 === Elizabeth daughter of Edward IV

James IV of Scotland (1st husband) === Margaret === Archibald Douglas (2nd husband)

Mary === Louis XII of France (1st husband)
=== Duke of Suffolk (2nd husband)

Marie Guise === James V of Scotland

Margaret === Matthew Stuart

Frances === Henry Grey

Francis II King of France (1st husband) === Mary Queen of Scots === Henry Stuart Lord Darnley (2nd husband)

Charles Stuart === Elizabeth Cavendish

Lady Jane Grey

James I 1603–1625 James VI of Scotland

Arabella Stuart

5

The young Henry VIII, plus (inset page 7) the older Henry.

Henry VIII

When Henry VII died, Henry VIII became king. Now it was his duty to get married and have male children. The sons were needed to carry on the Tudor line.

So the person Henry married might not be the person he fell in love with. This was difficult for Henry, who fell in love easily.

Henry was used to having his own way. In modern language we would call him a 'control freak'.

When Henry came to the throne at 18, he was an intelligent, handsome, sporting man. He was well educated and played musical instruments. He was 6 ft 2 in (1.88 m) – very tall for his time.

Henry was proud of his looks when he was young, but he got fat as he got older and developed illnesses, such as leg ulcers that would not heal. These made him cross and difficult. The young and old Henry were therefore very different people, as his wives discovered!

Did you know… ?

- Henry VIII was the first English king to insist on being called "Your Majesty".
- Henry was a 'ladies man', meaning he fell in love easily. He was not faithful and had a large number of **mistresses**.
- Henry had a fierce temper. When enraged, the king became "the most dangerous and cruel man in the world".
- As he grew older, the king became suspicious of everyone and he could easily turn on old friends and even have them executed. This made life in court very treacherous.

 How did Henry change as he got older?

Catherine of Aragon's story

My marriage to Arthur was decided when I was just three years old. This was the normal way of doing things and I grew up knowing that my fate was to one day become Queen of England. Of course, things did not end up the way I thought they would.

My parents were the most famous royal people in all of Europe. I was lucky, because this meant that, unlike most women, I was taught to read and write Latin and French and other subjects as well as the traditional wife's skills — embroidery, music, dance, drawing and cooking. As a **Catholic**, I was taught not only that God blessed a king's reign, but that any marriage between king and queen was God's will.

I went to England when I was 15 and Arthur and I were married in a grand ceremony. Just a few months later we both became very ill and Arthur died. I was very ill for a long time and when I recovered, the King of England and my parents decided that I should marry Arthur's brother, Henry. I did not know Henry very well, but I was very happy that I had a future. Henry was very tall and handsome and he loved hunting and other sports.

During Henry's first years as king, I often advised him and helped to run the country, but soon

continued...

Catherine of Aragon

Born:	1485
Married:	11th June 1509
Divorced/ annulled:	1533
Married for:	24 years
Died:	7th January 1536 (aged 50)
Life after divorce:	3 years

Cardinal Wolsey began to have the king's ear more and more, and I was given less and less to do with the affairs of state.

I looked forward to having a son who would grow up to be King of England, but it was not to be. I had many pregnancies, but only one child who lived. Doctors said that the **miscarriages** might have been caused by my long illness.

Many years went by and I know that Henry was seeing other women, but I kept quiet as a dignified queen should. Then Henry became very unhappy and asked me for a divorce, but as a good Catholic, I do not believe in divorce. Then he asked the Pope to convince me to join a **convent**. That way, I would be married to God and my marriage to Henry could be cancelled. But if I did that, Mary, my daughter, would never be queen. When I found out that Henry had asked the Pope for the marriage to be cancelled, I knew I had to act.

Luckily, the Pope is good friends with my nephew, King Charles I of Spain, so the Pope took my side and refused to cancel the marriage. But Henry was listening to Wolsey and to his Archbishop, Thomas Cranmer. They were greedy for power. Cranmer convinced Henry that he, and not the Pope,

continued...

should be head of the Church in England. That way, he could make any religious rules he liked. Cranmer declared that our marriage was against God's law, because I had been married to his brother, Arthur, first.

I was told that I had no choice but to accept the divorce and let Henry marry Anne Boleyn. But I refused – I did not believe in divorce and I would not give up Mary's claim to the throne. Even though Henry had already married Anne Boleyn, I refused to give her my crown jewels. I told Henry that his new wife was the scandal of Christendom and a disgrace to him. Because I refused to co-operate, Henry made Mary and me live in one draughty old castle after another.

I always refused to let anyone use my new title "Dowager Princess of Wales" and ignored anyone who did not address me as queen. From time to time, the king sent royal envoys to have me swear the oath that recognised Henry's marriage to Anne Boleyn as lawful. I always told them, "I am queen and queen I will die."

Anne Boleyn's story

My life began in a very normal way for a lady of noble birth. When I was 12 years old, I was sent to be a lady-in-waiting at the court of the Archduchess Margaret. Being a lady-in-waiting is how high-born girls are taught how to behave at court. As a lady-in-waiting I had a chance to learn all about art, music, dance, conversation and how to be the wife of a nobleman. It was expected that I would marry a nobleman.

After a few years with Margaret, I was sent to the household of Mary Tudor, who was married to Louis XII, King of France. I loved France and soon learned to speak and read French and to love French art, music and clothes. When I was 20, I was told to return to England, to wait on Queen Catherine, because my parents were arranging for my marriage to the son of the Duke of Ormonde.

The plans for my marriage fell through and I began looking around for another rich nobleman to marry. But living at court, I soon attracted the attention of the king. I decided immediately that I would like to be queen, but I had to be careful. Henry was still married, and he had a lot of other mistresses, but he promised that as soon as his

continued...

Anne Boleyn

Born:	1500
Married:	January 1533
Married for:	3 years
Executed:	19th May 1536 (aged 36)

marriage to Catherine was cancelled by the Pope, he would marry me. The years dragged on, I became tired of waiting for the divorce. Every time I got angry at waiting, Henry would buy me more jewellery and clothes as gifts to make me feel better, but after more than six years of waiting, I became **pregnant** and Henry decided he had to marry me. Of course, the ceremony had to be kept secret.

After the divorce to Catherine finally happened, I was crowned on 1 June, 1533, at Westminster Abbey. As we rode in a magnificent procession from the Tower of London to Westminster, Londoners cried "HA! HA!" as a joke on our initials – Henry and Anne. It seems that the people loved Catherine of Aragon and hated me.

Although Henry was pleased to have our child – Elizabeth – I know he was disappointed it wasn't a boy. I was disappointed as well. I knew only too well that I had many enemies at court and the only way to remain queen was to give Henry a son, but after two more miscarriages, Henry grew tired of waiting for a boy. He began to see my maid-of-honour Jane Seymour, and my enemies decided to act against me.

I had made many enemies at court because of my support for the **Reformers**. My worst enemy was Thomas Cromwell, who had always resented my influence over the king.

continued...

My maids were pressured, under pain of torture I have no doubt, into telling stories about me having men into my bed chamber at late hours and I was charged with conspiracy to murder the king and adultery with four men: my favourite musician, Mark Smeaton, and other men were also charged. The worst was the charge of making love to my own brother George. This was simply untrue, but his wife was jealous of me and so she gave false evidence against us.

I was tried on made up charges of **adultery**. They were all lies, but it didn't matter, adultery by the queen is **treason**, and in a treason trial there can be no defence. I am only sorry that so many innocent men had to die with me. Of course, they would not have been charged if they, too, had not also made many enemies at court. That is how life is at court. One day you are the king's favourite, the next day your enemies have won and you have lost your head.

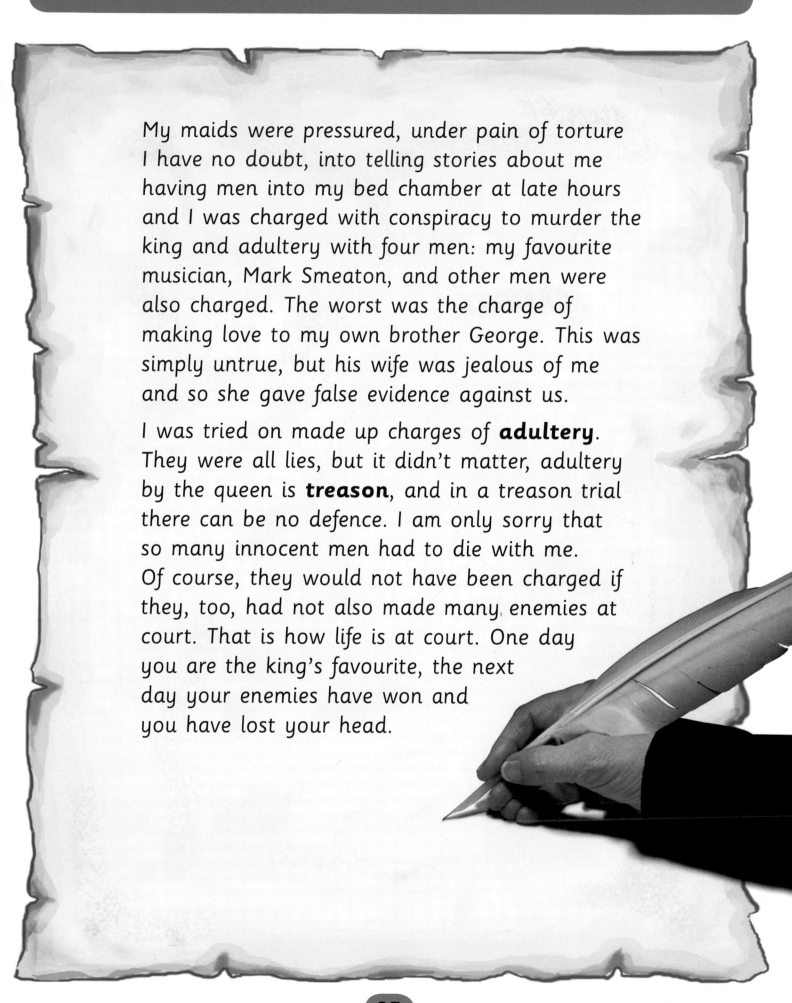

Jane Seymour's story

My parents always taught me that a proper lady should be silent, obedient and sweet-tempered. They did not approve of education for women and so I did not learn to read and write more than my name. Instead, I was taught wifely skills of household management and needlework. But when I was at court, as maid-of-honour to Queen Catherine and to Anne Boleyn, I also learned the ways of getting along at court.

I had been at court for six years as maid-of-honour to Catherine of Aragon and Anne Boleyn when the king began to pay attention to me. As he was still married, I refused to make love to him, but this only made him want me more. When it became obvious that the king was interested in me, those who were against Anne Boleyn, and especially those who were still Catholics, rushed to my side to help me.

Because I am a good Catholic and do not approve of the Reformation, they hoped that I would encourage the king to return to the 'true faith' and give up Reform.

After we were married, I helped Henry and his elder daughter, Mary, to get together again. Mary was a good Catholic, like me, and my hope was that

continued...

Jane Seymour

Born: 1509
Married: 30th May 1536
Married for: 1 year
Died: 24th October 1537
               (aged 27)

◄ ③ **Prince Edward (later Edward VI).**

Mary could eventually become queen and end the Reformation. When rebellions broke out in 1536, and the people demanded the restoration of the Catholic Church, I tried to convince the king to listen, but Henry exploded with anger and reminded me of what had happened to his other queens, so I learned my place and did not interfere in the affairs of state.

After I became pregnant, the king made sure I had everything I could want. Once I had a craving for quails, and so Henry had some shipped all the way from Calais in France.

On 12 October, 1537, I gave birth to a son – Edward. I had been in labour for three days. Although I felt good, if a bit weak, after the birth, I soon took ill with a fever, which was very common. When the end came for me, I had been queen for just 18 months, but I had fulfilled the greatest task of a Tudor queen, I had given the king a male heir.

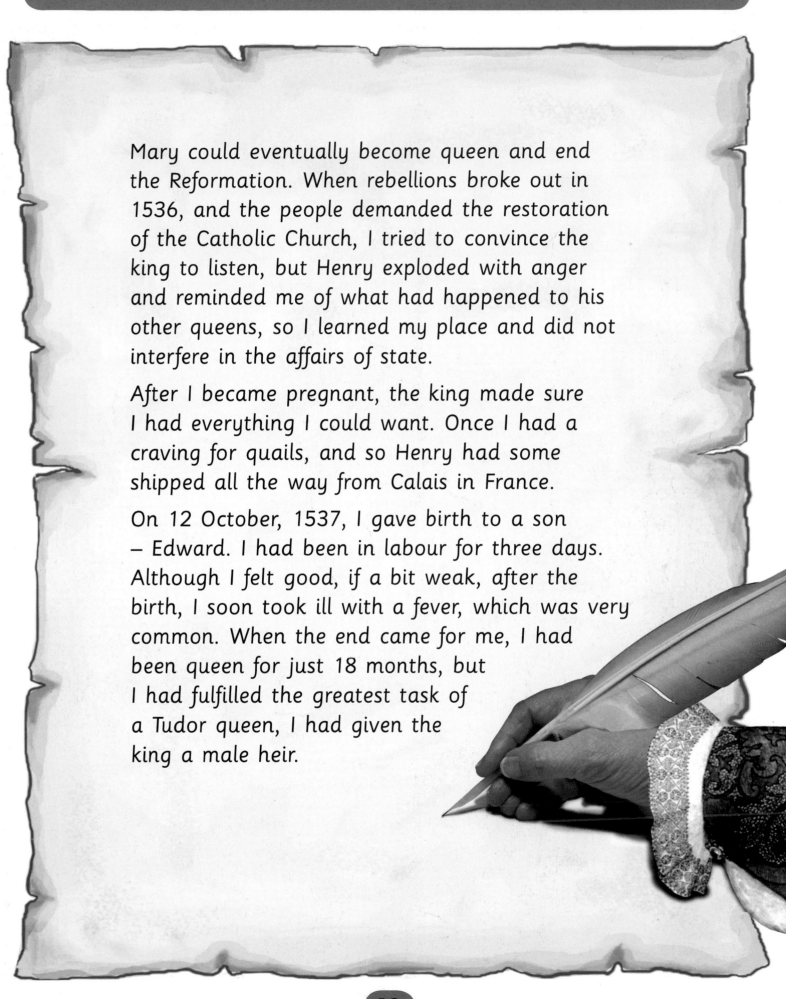

Anne of Cleves' story

As a noblewoman, living in difficult times, I always knew that my parents would arrange a political match for me, but I was very surprised when I learned that someone as grand as the King of England wanted me to be his wife. Of course, I was honoured, although I was also worried. After all, everyone knew what had happened to his first two wives. So, before I left for England, I determined that I would always act as a good wife should. I would not get involved in politics and I would be honourable and good.

I was very excited to arrive in England, because I had not been away from my homeland before, but you can imagine my disappointment when Henry let everyone know how unhappy he was with me. I know I am not the most prettiest of women, and in Cleve we do not use fancy perfumes to disguise our strong body odour, but I still thought that the king would be happy with me. I did not expect that Henry would try to break off our engagement and that after our marriage he would be unwilling to share our marriage bed, even for one night. I have to say that I did not find Henry attractive

continued...

Anne of Cleves

Born:	1515
Married:	6th January 1540
Divorced:	1540
Married for:	1 year
Died:	16th July 1557 (aged 42)
Life after divorce:	17 years

either, but all the same I was determined to be a faithful wife.

My life at court was very difficult. I had been raised to be a good wife and had not been taught music, singing or dancing, which many of the women at Henry's court knew well. I also did not speak any English, Latin or French, but I was famous for my skill at needlework, which made many people think highly of me, and I engaged a tutor to teach me English. I also made sure to never drink alcohol, or to give anyone a reason to tell tales about me.

Although the king did not want to be married to me, I played the good wife. I appeared at some public events, and spent my days playing cards with my ladies-in-waiting, learning English, and working on my needlework. I hoped that in time I could convince the king to have me crowned in a coronation and secure my place as queen.

Because I did not speak English well, I could not understand the gossip at court and it was several months before I heard the rumours of the king's interest in Kathryn Howard. I remembered what had happened to Catherine and Anne, and so when the king asked me to agree to an end to my marriage,

continued...

I did it without hesitation. After all, it is better to be alive and not be queen, than to be dead.

But because I had never given the king any cause to dislike me, he rewarded my co-operation with a rank as the second lady in the kingdom after any future queen – even before the king's daughters. I was also given a rich collection of estates and manors that provided me with a handsome yearly income. I simply had to agree not to leave England. I was to bear the title of the 'King's Sister'. In this way the king kept the good connections of my family but was free to marry again. As for me, I was then 25, wealthy and free, something I soon learned to enjoy. You see, I had never been in love with the king, so I did not miss him.

I enjoyed a life of leisure and spent my time at cards, games and masques. I even learned to drink alcohol. I remained good friends with the king and his new wife, Kathryn Howard, and entertained them at dinner often. Of course, I never married again.

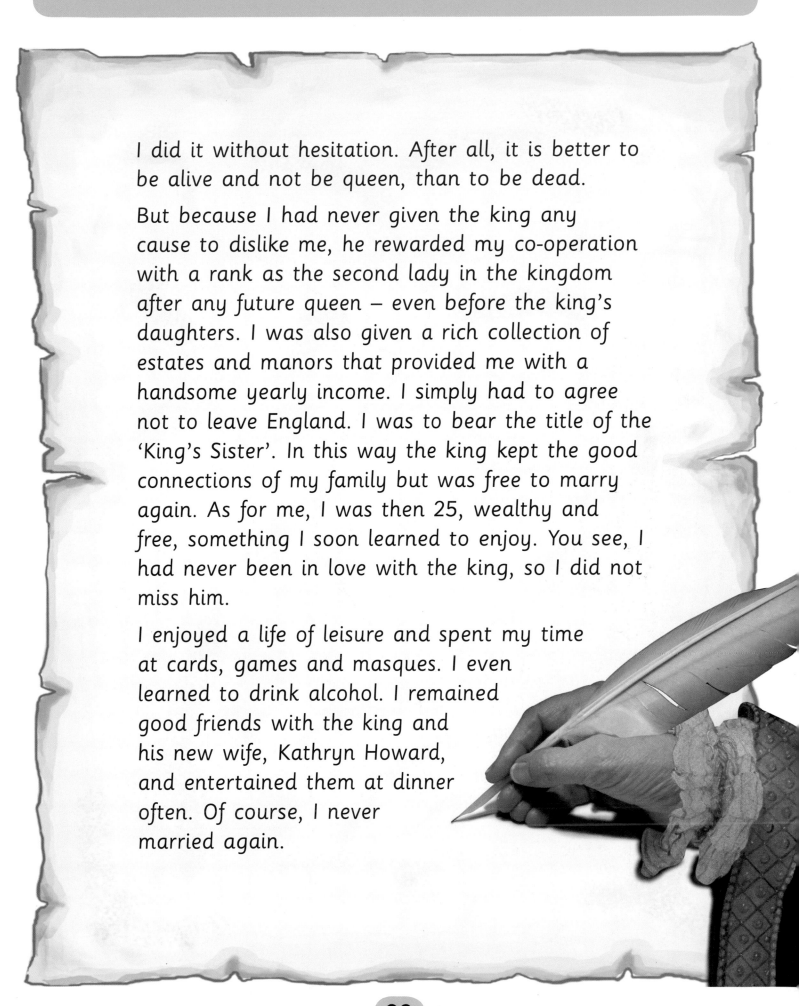

Kathryn Howard's story

My parents came from a noble and powerful family. But not all of my family were rich. In fact my father was poor because he was a younger son of the Duke of Norfolk, not the heir to the family fortune. This is why, at an early age, I was sent to live with my step-grandmother, Agnes, Dowager Duchess of Norfolk. The Duchess of Norfolk had been a very important woman at court when she was younger and my parents hoped that she would help me to win the heart of a wealthy young nobleman with good connections.

The Duchess had a lovely and comfortable house at Lambeth near London and she arranged for me to learn to read, write and to play music — important skills at Henry's court. She was not very strict, so I was able to do the things I loved best — flirt with boys and make merry. In fact, I made merry with two much older men while I lived with the Duchess and she never knew.

When I was 15, the Duchess arranged for me to start my life at court as maid-of-honour to Anne of Cleves. I loved life at court. It was so glamorous and luxurious and there were so many handsome men!

continued...

SVÆ ·21

Kathryn Howard

Born:	1521
Married:	28th July 1540
Married for:	1 year. 6 months
Executed:	13th February 1542 (aged 21)

But the court was home to the king. It was not long before he caught my eye, or was it the other way around? I don't remember. He was certainly not young or handsome, but fat and with an ulcerated leg. I did not mind, because he was king and he gave me all sorts of wonderful and beautiful gifts. All I had to do was laugh and flirt and I knew that I could be queen.

But being queen was not as much fun as I thought it would be. I cared for Henry and we had fun together, even though he was old and the ulcer on his leg was a bit disgusting and smelly.

When Henry was sad and cross, I dutifully attended him. I ignored the pus-oozing ulcers on his leg and he rewarded me with his love and with many gifts.

I did not meddle in Henry's political affairs and had no interest in religious issues. I was really only interested in having fun, and with so many young men around, there were so many opportunities.

Eventually, I was found out. It was one of my family's enemies, Archbishop Cranmer, who told the king about my affairs. He hated my family

continued...

because we are Catholics and he is a Reformer and he was always looking for evidence against me. I suppose it wasn't too hard to find. At first, I hoped the king would forgive me, but there was too much evidence. At first, I panicked, but then decided that I would at least die with dignity.

The night before my execution I had the executioner's block brought to me so that I could rehearse for my final appearance as queen. Throughout the night, I practised placing my head on the block, for I was determined to die with dignity and composure. Although so weak I could barely stand, I managed to make a short speech in which I admitted I was justly condemned, prayed for the king and asked for God's mercy.

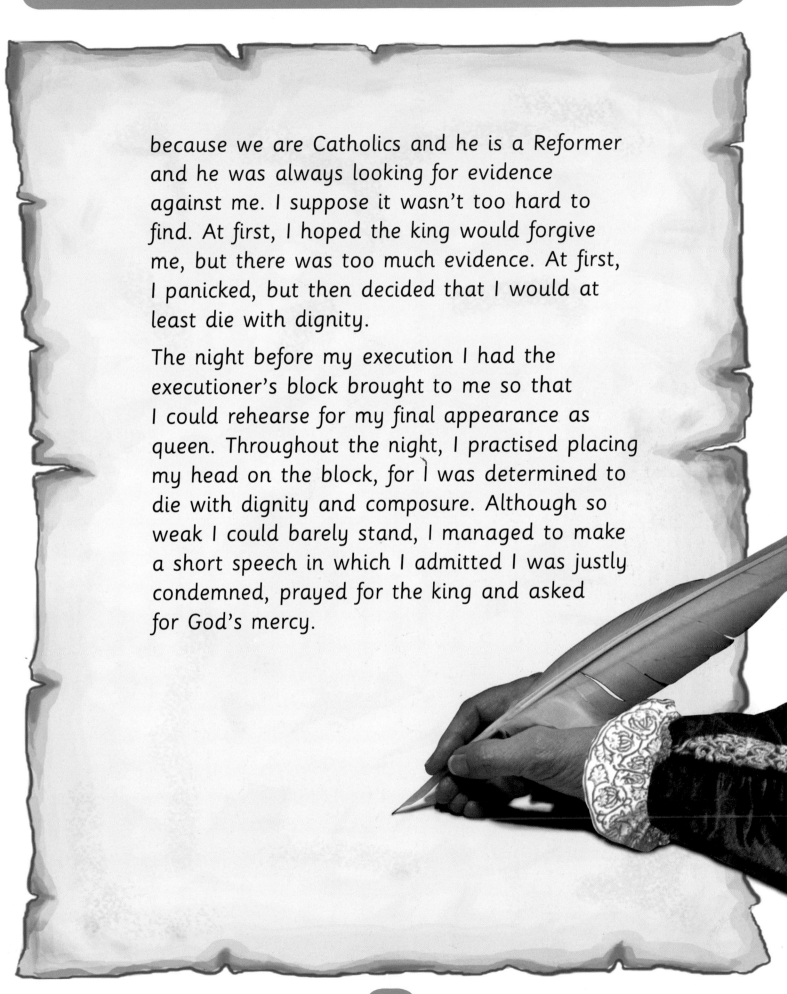

Katherine Parr's story

I have never expected to be queen, especially at the late age of 31, and already twice married and widowed. But Henry and I had known each other since I was a child. My father and Henry were old friends and I think he turned to me as a trusted and true nursemaid. When Henry asked me to marry him, I already had a marriage understanding with Sir Thomas Seymour, younger brother of the late Queen Jane. But I put aside love for duty, for when the king asks for your hand in marriage, it does not do to say no.

My duty as queen was clear, to play nurse to the king and to act as a traditional queen – speaking with ambassadors, entertaining at court, and setting an example for the people by being trustworthy and true. In truth, the king was not demanding of me, I was not expected to have any children, but to be a companion to the king. I also took Henry's children under my care. They had too long been denied a mother's love and care, and I was anxious that they did not grow up wild because of this.

continued...

HARINE PARRE

Katherine Parr

Born: 1512
Married: 12ᵗʰ July 1543
Widowed: 28ᵗʰ January 1547
Died: 5ᵗʰ September 1548
Life after
Henry: 1 year

I had been brought up as a Protestant and I hoped that my time at court would influence the king and country more in that direction. I had been given a great deal of education by my mother, more than most women receive, and I was used to leading scholarly debates.

Unfortunately, the king was tired and had lost interest in church reform and I fell foul of Lord Chancellor Thomas Wriothesley, and his campaign to wipe out so-called "heretics". Wriothesley led a conservative group who wished to turn the country back towards Catholicism and they saw me as an obstacle to this.

The king and I often passed the time in religious discussion and one day the anti-reform Bishop Stephen Gardiner, a firm friend of Wriothesley, overheard a most vigorous religious argument between us. Gardiner warned Henry against harbouring "a serpent within his own bosom," and convinced Henry to sign a warrant for my arrest on grounds of **heresy**.

A servant loyal to me gave me a copy of the warrant. At first I panicked, and then I realised what I had to do to survive. While my ladies-in-waiting burned all the banned books on religion I had collected in my room, I hurried to the king.

continued...

Henry steered the conversation to religion, commenting that "ye are become a doctor, Kate, to instruct us . . .," but I had the perfect response. I replied, "I am but a woman, with all the imperfections natural to the weakness of my sex; therefore in all matters of doubt and difficulty I must refer myself to your Majesty's better judgement, as to my lord and head".

My submissiveness worked. When that fool Wriothesley next came to see the king, he was greeted with cries from the king of "Knave!," "Fool!" and "Beast!" The warrant was dropped and I was given a set of gorgeous new jewels for my loyalty.

When the king died, I was sad, for he had been a good husband to me, but I had done my duty and my life at court was over. Once my period of mourning was over, I was free to marry Seymour and once again live my own life.

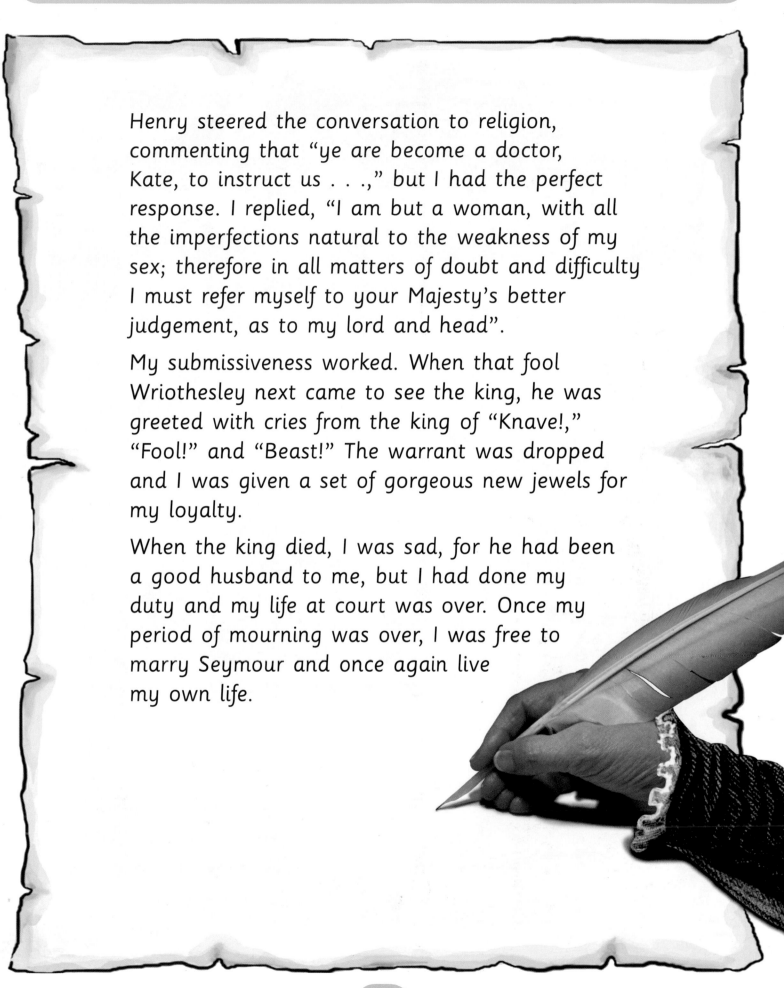

Glossary

adultery Making love to a husband or wife to whom you are not married.

Catholic, Roman Catholic Part of the Christian church whose head is the Pope in Rome.

civil war A war between two groups of people who belong to the same country. Usually a civil war is a fight over who should succeed to the throne.

convent A religious house for nuns. Nuns are said to be married to Christ and so cannot also be married to a man.

heresy Something said or written against the teachings of the church.

miscarriage When a mother has a baby that is born dead. This usually happens when the baby is very small and long before it would normally have been born.

mistress A women who is not married to a man, but who is almost like a second wife. However, a mistress is never openly acknowledged.

noble People who belonged to rich and powerful families and who have titles given by the king.

pregnant To carry a child.

Reformers People who thought that the Catholic Church had lost its way and become too much to do with ritual. They were also called Protestants because they protested against the way the Catholic Church behaved.

treason Doing something which will threaten the country's welfare. In Tudor times the country was the king.

Tudor The kings and queens who made up the royal line starting with Henry VII and ending with Elizabeth I (because she was childless).

Index

Curriculum Visions

Curriculum Visions Explorers
This series provides straightforward introductions to key worlds and ideas.

You might also be interested in
Our slightly more detailed book, 'In the Queen's words: Discovering what the wives of Henry VIII thought'. There is a Teacher's Guide to match 'In the Queen's words'. Additional notes in PDF format are also available from the publisher to support 'Exploring the lives of Henry VIII's wives'. All of these products are suitable for KS2.

Dedicated Web Site
Watch movies, see many more pictures and read much more in detail about life in Tudor times at:

www.curriculumvisions.com
(Professional Zone: subscription required)

A CVP Book
Copyright © 2007 Earthscape

Authors
Brian Knapp, BSc, PhD and Lisa Magloff, MA

Educational Consultant
JM Smith (former Deputy Head of Wellfield School, Burnley, Lancashire)

Senior Designer
Adele Humphries, BA

Editor
Gillian Gatehouse

Photographs
The Earthscape Picture Library, except *TopFoto* cover, pages 2, 4, 6, 7, 9, 13, 17, 18, 21, 25, 29.

Designed and produced by
Earthscape

Printed in China by
WKT Company Ltd

Exploring the lives of Henry VIII's wives – Curriculum Visions
A CIP record for this book is available from the British Library
ISBN 978 1 86214 215 2

This product is manufactured from sustainable managed forests. For every tree cut down at least one more is planted.